Children's Press®
A Division of Scholastic Inc.
New York   Toronto   London   Auckland
Mexico City   New Delhi   Hong Kong
Danbury, Connecticut

W9-COJ-603

Designer: Herman Adler Design
Photo Researcher: Caroline Anderson
The photo on the cover shows a boy looking at a bruise on his leg.

Library of Congress Cataloging-in-Publication Data

Gordon, Sharon.
    Bruises / by Sharon Gordon.
      p. cm. — (Rookie read-about health)
    Includes index.
    Summary: Provides a brief introduction to bruises explaining how they
form and how they heal.
    ISBN 0-516-22568-5 (lib. bdg.)   0-516-26872-4 (pbk.)
    1. Bruises—Juvenile literature. [1. Bruises. 2. Wounds and injuries.]
I. Title. II. Series.
RD96.15.G67   2002
617.1'3—dc21

                                       2001002690

Hey, watch out!

You just bumped into me.

That bump might turn into
a bruise.

A bruise is different from a cut.

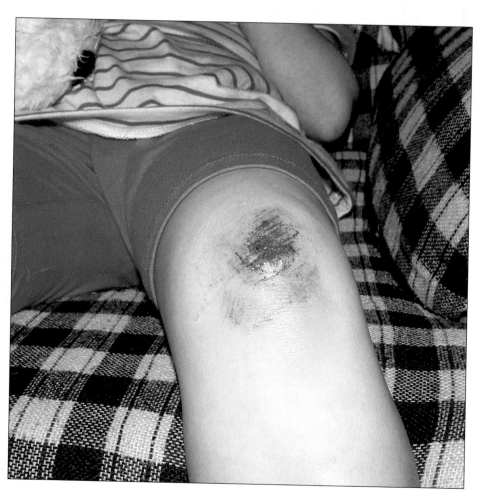

The skin on a bruise is
not broken. No blood
can come out.

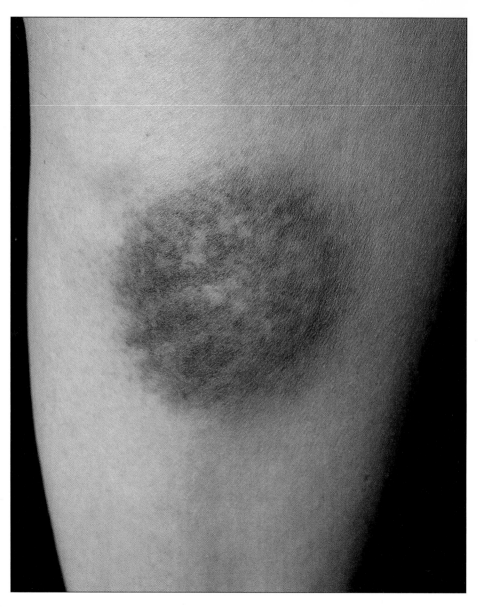

8

The blood stays trapped under your skin. That is what gives a bruise its dark color.

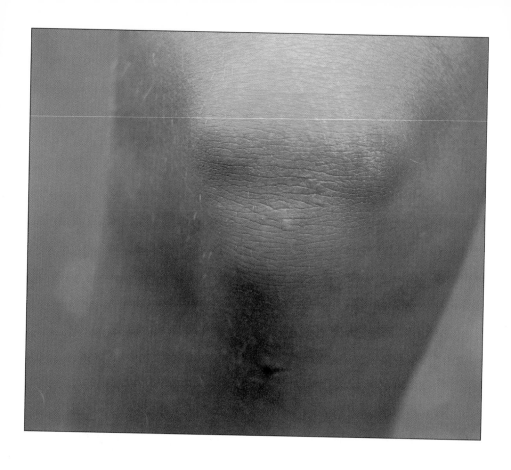

Sometimes a bruise
gets puffy. It might
feel a little sore.

You can put ice on a very bad bruise. That will help keep the swelling down.

Sometimes, we call bruises "black and blue" marks. That is the color your skin might turn when it is bruised.

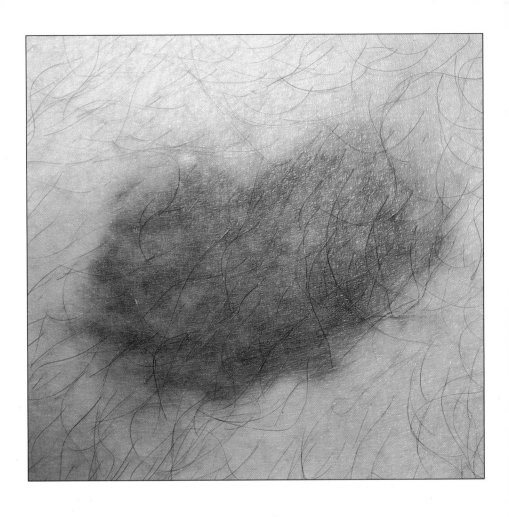

Other bruises might
look purple.

14

If you get bumped hard,
you will have a dark
bruise. A smaller bump
will make a lighter bruise.

People with lighter skin
have lighter bruises.
The darker the skin, the
darker the bruises look.

Bruises take a while to heal, or get better.

The purple mark starts to fade. It might turn green or yellow. The puffiness goes down.

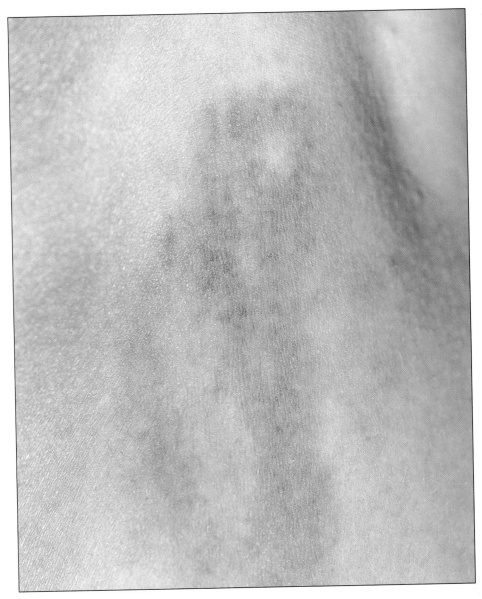

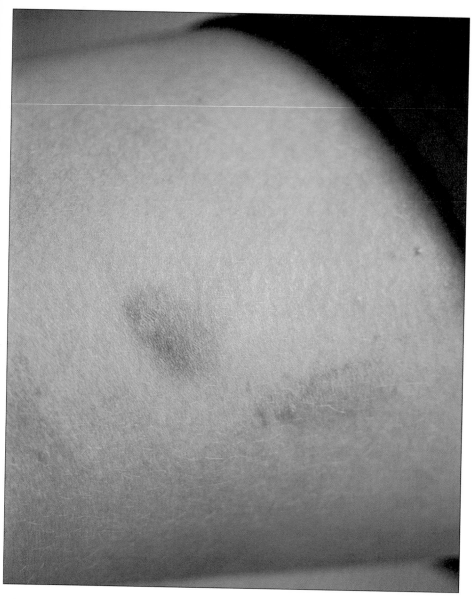

18

The bruise gets lighter and lighter each day.

You can hardly see where it was!

All of us get bruises
from time to time.
We trip and fall.

We get hit by the ball!

Always be careful where you walk.

Watch where you are going.

It is important to follow safety rules.

Put on your helmet.

And don't forget the kneepads!

Open drawers are a real danger.

And so is a wet floor.
Oh no! Don't slip!

Remember to read the sign!

Words You Know

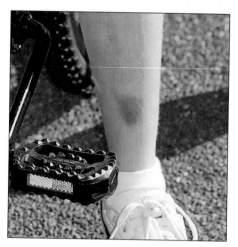

bruise

bump

fall

ice

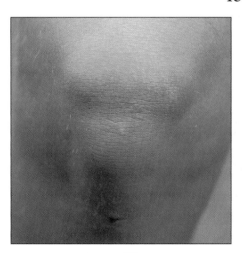

puffy

safety rules

Index

About the Author

Sharon Gordon is a writer living in Midland Park, New Jersey. She and her husband have three school-aged children and a spoiled pooch. Together they enjoy visiting the Outer Banks of North Carolina as often as possible.

Photo Credits